Step-by-Step
Papier Mâché

Judy Balchin

Search Press

First published in Great Britain 2000

Search Press Limited
Wellwood, North Farm Road,
Tunbridge Wells, Kent TN2 3DR

Text copyright © Judy Balchin 2000

Photographs by Search Press Studios
Photographs and design copyright © Search Press Ltd. 2000

ISBN 0 85532 912 2

Suppliers
If you have difficulty in obtaining any of the materials and equipment mentioned in this book, then please visit the Search Press website for details of suppliers: www.searchpress.com

Alternatively, you can write to the Publishers at the address above, for a current list of stockists, which includes firms who operate a mail-order service.

Acknowledgements
The Publishers would like to thank Christie's Images Ltd. for permission to reproduce the photograph on page 5.

Colour separation by Graphics '91 Pte Ltd., Singapore
Printed in Italy by L.E.G.O.

To my husband John. Here's to the next twenty-five years!

A big thank you to John Wright of Pebeo UK Ltd., Unit 109, Solent Business Centre, Millbrook Road West, Millbrook, Southampton, SO15 OHW for supplying the majority of the paints used in this book.

My thanks also to the team at Search Press, whose constant encouragement and sense of humour made the writing of this book a pleasure – in particular, Editorial Director Roz Dace, Editor Chantal Roser, Designer Tamsin Hayes and Photographer Lotti de la Bédoyère.

The Publishers would like to say a huge thank you to Jessika Kwan, Rheanna Wood, Letitia Thomas, Richard Pulsford, Mishelle Wallace, Joanna Hall, Robert Sharma and Brandon Pitchers.

Finally, special thanks to Southborough Primary School, Tunbridge Wells.

When this sign is used in the book, it means that adult supervision is needed.

REMEMBER!
Ask an adult to help you when you see this sign.

Contents

Introduction 4

Materials 6

Techniques 8

Celtic Goblet 12

Indian Frame 14

Native American
Headdress 16

Mexican Bowl 18

Gothic Mirror 20

Egyptian Cat 22

Aztec Necklace 24

Roman Box 26

African Pencil Pot 28

Patterns 30

Index 32

Introduction

Papier mâché is a French term which means 'chewed or mashed paper'. It was first invented in China in the first part of the second century. The Chinese discovered that it was possible to make many items out of papier mâché – they created pots and even warrior helmets which they then covered with a varnish to make them hard-wearing and durable. Over time, mankind became more and more ambitious, and by the seventeenth century even a church was being built using papier mâché! In the following century, a man called Charles Ducrest drew up plans for making tables, bookcases and even houses, boats and bridges using either papier mâché on its own, or wood or iron structures covered in papier mâché.

Although you will not be making churches, houses or boats in this book, you will be able to have lots of fun with papier mâché – from making a simple photograph frame to modelling a cat. I have taken the inspiration for the items from past civilisations. You will be taken on a journey to discover Celtic and Indian decoration, Native American, Mexican and Gothic design, Egyptian, Aztec, Roman and African art.

There are two main ways of making papier mâché: layering and pulping. You will be using both methods in the projects in this book, sometimes combining both on one piece. Each project shows you a different way of using papier mâché and suggests how you can decorate your pieces.

If you are interested in recycling rubbish, then this book is definitely for you. Old newspapers, cardboard tubing and sweet wrappers are just a few of the things that you will be working with, so start hoarding! Before you throw anything away, ask yourself if it could be used in a papier mâché project. An old plastic bottle or cardboard box can spark off an amazing idea, so keep your eyes open. In particular, watch out for coloured papers, beads, feathers, string and foil papers . . . in fact anything that could be used to decorate your creations.

We all like to make things, but to make something totally unique has a special meaning. As you become more confident using papier mâché, I am sure you will come up with lots of your own ideas and designs. Be bold, experiment, but most of all, have lots of fun.

Opposite *Many people think that papier mâché is used only by children to make simple and inexpensive items like masks. However, this richly decorated box, called a casket, was made from papier mâché in the 1770s. It must have been bought by a very wealthy or important person, because it would have cost a great deal of money to decorate it so beautifully.*

5

Materials

The best thing about papier mâché is that it is such a cheap hobby. You will not need all the things listed on this page to begin. Many of the materials that you need to get started can be found in your own home. Keep a box handy so that you can store old newspapers, tissue and coloured paper, cardboard boxes and tubes. All these will come in handy for papier mâché projects.

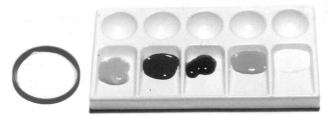

White emulsion paint is used to prime a surface before decorating with coloured paint. The coloured paint used in this book is acrylic. This paint covers well and is hard-wearing. Poster paint can also be used, but this needs to be protected with a coat of varnish. Varnish can also be used to give a shiny appearance. It is best to use paint from a palette rather than straight from the pot.

Sheets of newspaper can be used to cover your work surface. Strips of newspaper are used for the basic layering technique. Paper pulp is used for modelling or applying to a surface for a textured look. You can buy it in packs at craft shops or make your own from pieces of newspaper (see page 10).

Paint can be applied with a paintbrush. An assortment of sizes are used in this book. The end of a paintbrush can be used to make holes in the pulp. A piece of sponge can also be used to apply paint. A toothbrush is used for spattering paint and a potato is used to stamp paint on to a surface.

You will need a selection of bowls, a colander or sieve, wooden spoon, tablespoon and mug for making pulp and mixing up wallpaper paste. A cooling rack is ideal for drying pieces on. Clingfilm is used to seal bowls containing made-up wallpaper paste. It can also be used to line a mould before it is covered with paper pulp.

Non-toxic wallpaper paste is used for all papier mâché work. PVA glue is added to wallpaper paste to strengthen the mix. It can also be used as a glue. If you dilute PVA glue with water to the consistency of thin cream, it can be used as a varnish. It should be applied with a paste brush. Always wash your hands after handling glue and wallpaper paste.

Scissors are used to cut paper, thin card and string. A **craft knife** is used to cut thick corrugated card. Always ask an adult to do this for you as craft knives are very sharp. Craft knives should be used on a **cutting board**. A **vegetable knife** is used to cut a shape in a potato so that you can print with it.

Thin card (for example, from a cereal packet) is ideal as a base for many papier mâché projects. **Cardboard** is also used. This comes in different thicknesses – single and double corrugated cardboard are used in this book. Cardboard boxes are fine to use. **Cardboard tubing** comes in different widths, and this is also used.

A **ruler** and **pencil** are used for measuring pieces of cardboard and drawing straight lines. A pencil is also used to trace around patterns.

Masking tape is used to hold pieces of card in position before applying pasted newspaper strips. It is also used for masking off areas from paint.

Beads, feathers, ribbon, string and **glass droplets** are all used for decoration. Beads can be threaded on to **leather thong. Coloured foil paper** can be glued to a surface for a sparkly look or scrunched into balls and used as jewel-like decorations. Old sweet wrappers are ideal.

Techniques

Papier mâché is not a difficult craft, but it is worth reading through this techniques section carefully before you begin the projects.

Note Papier mâché is messy so it is best to cover your workspace with a large piece of newspaper. Alternatively, use polythene – this can be wiped down and used again.

Transferring a design on to cardboard

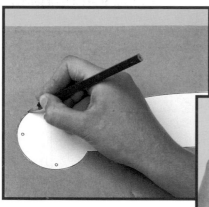

Patterns are provided at the end of the book. These can be enlarged on a photocopier. Cut around the photocopied pattern, then lay it on thin card or single corrugated cardboard and run round the edge with a pencil. Cut around the line with scissors.

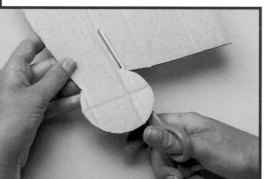

(!) Double corrugated cardboard is much tougher than single, and it needs to be cut with a craft knife. Ask an adult to do this for you as craft knives are very sharp.

Preventing warping

Sometimes, papier mâché pieces made from a cardboard base can warp during the drying process. To prevent this, always give your base cardboard shape a coat of slightly diluted PVA glue.

Paste both sides of the cardboard then leave to dry naturally on a cooling rack, turning occasionally so that it dries evenly. When completely dry, the cardboard can be layered with newspaper strips (see opposite).

Note When PVA glue is dry, it can be very difficult to remove so wear an apron or old shirt to protect your clothes.

Mixing up the paste

Pour half a litre (one pint) of water into a bowl and sprinkle with wallpaper paste (the instructions on the packet will tell you how much to use). Stir the mixture well, leave it for fifteen minutes, then add a tablespoon of PVA glue to strengthen the paste.

Note Once wallpaper paste has been made up, it can be stored in a bowl fitted with an airtight lid or sealed with clingfilm. It will last for several days if kept in the fridge.

Layering with newspaper strips

Layering involves pasting strips of newspaper with a mixture of wallpaper paste and PVA glue, and then sticking them on to a base. When dry, the pieces will be strong but light, and ready for decorating.

Tear small strips of newspaper for small structures, and larger strips for bigger items. Use your fingers to smear paste on to the strips of paper then press them on to your base so that they overlap each other. Smooth the strips down as you work.

Note Complete one layer at a time. You will be told how many layers to apply for each project. To help you keep count of the number of layers you have worked, you can apply one layer of coloured newspaper, then one layer of black and white and so on.

Using paper pulp

Papier mâché pulp can be bought from art shops. It is a powdered paper which is mixed with water to create a modelling material. You can also make your own, as shown here. Once you have mixed up the pulp, it can be stored in a polythene bag in the fridge until needed.

1 Tear enough small pieces of newspaper to fill a mug when packed tightly.

 Place the pieces of newspaper in a bowl and cover with hot water. Leave to soak for three hours.

 Transfer the soaked paper into a colander or sieve. Squeeze the pieces together so that the water runs out and the paper forms a mash.

4 Put the mash into a bowl and add a tablespoon of PVA glue and a tablespoon of wallpaper paste mixture (see page 9).

5 Mix everything together with your fingers.

Note When you have completed a pulped papier mâché project, leave it to dry naturally. The pulp shrinks as it dries and sometimes creates small splits or cracks in the surface. These can be disguised by smearing a little more paper pulp into them and allowing this to dry again.

Priming and painting

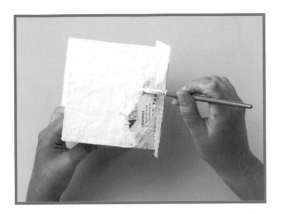

Priming means preparing a surface so that it can then be decorated with coloured paint. Use white emulsion paint to do this. You may need two coats to cover the newspaper print completely. Allow the first coat to dry before applying the second.

The projects in this book are decorated with acrylic paint as it covers well, is hard-wearing and does not need to be varnished. Once the white primer is dry, paint your finished object in colours of your choice.

Note All items painted with poster paint should be protected with a coat of varnish — you can use diluted PVA glue for this. If you do use poster paint, mix it with a little PVA glue before you apply it. This will prevent the paint from smearing when you varnish it.

Celtic Goblet

Celtic craftsmen were well-known for their metal work. The goblet in this project is made to look like metal, but it is actually made out of an old plastic drinks bottle. The surface is covered with pulp to create a textured surface which looks like beaten metal. It is decorated with metallic paint and glass droplets to create a container that is truly fit for a king! Remember that this goblet is purely decorative and can not be used to drink out of.

YOU WILL NEED

Plastic drinks bottle
Single corrugated cardboard
Paper pulp • Glass droplets
Metallic acrylic paint
Paintbrush • Palette • PVA glue
Scissors • Masking tape
Newspaper

 Cut off the top third of a plastic drinks bottle.

 Cut a circle of single corrugated cardboard approximately 6.5cm (2½in) in diameter. Use masking tape to attach the cardboard circle to the top of the bottle.

3 Cover the outside of the plastic bottle and the cardboard base with a layer of pulp.

Note The pulp may dry on your fingers as you work. Keep a bowl of water next to you so that you can wet your fingers occasionally to stop this from happening.

Neaten the rim of the goblet by pressing the pulp onto the plastic edge.

5 While the pulp is still wet, put a blob of PVA glue on the back of eight glass droplets and then press them firmly into the pulp around the goblet. Leave to dry for forty-eight hours.

6 Paint the inside and outside of the goblet with metallic acrylic paint.

FURTHER IDEAS

Decorate your goblet using buttons or small pebbles instead of glass droplets.

Indian Frame

The shape of this Indian frame was inspired by the domed roof of the Taj Mahal, a beautiful tomb in India which was built by a Mogul Emperor for his wife. The decoration for the frame is based on Indian saris – these are made of brightly coloured cloth and metallic threads. I have used sweet wrappers and metallic paint in this project to transform a plain piece of cardboard into a frame to treasure.

YOU WILL NEED
Coloured foil sweet wrappers
Double corrugated cardboard
Thin card • Newspaper
Wallpaper paste • PVA glue • Paste brush
Metallic and coloured acrylic paint
Sponge • Palette • Pencil
Scissors • Craft knife • String
Masking tape

(!) Double corrugated cardboard needs to be cut with a craft knife. Ask an adult to do this for you as craft knives are very sharp.

1 Photocopy and enlarge the pattern on page 31 (see page 30) then cut it out and place it on to a piece of double corrugated cardboard. Trace around the pattern with a pencil then cut out the cardboard frame.

2 Paste both sides of the cardboard frame with PVA glue diluted with a little water. Leave to dry. Apply two layers of pasted newspaper strips to the front then leave to dry for a couple of hours.

3 Tear foil sweet wrappers into irregular shapes. Paste the back of each piece with PVA glue then press them on to the cardboard frame. Cover the front and the edges. Overlap the foil pieces on to the back. Leave to dry.

4 Pour a little metallic acrylic paint on to a palette. Dip a piece of sponge into the paint then dab it on to the outer and inner edges of the frame. Leave to dry.

Paint the back of the frame in a colour of your choice. Leave to dry. Cut out a piece of thin card, slightly bigger than the opening in the frame. Cut a wide 'v' shape in the top of the card. Tape the card over the opening, leaving the top un-taped – this will create a pocket for your picture or photograph.

FURTHER IDEAS

Create a different effect by decorating your frame with torn pieces of coloured tissue paper.

6 Tape a loop of string to the back of the frame for hanging. Insert your picture or photograph.

Native American Headdress

A war bonnet decorated with eagle feathers is the mark of an experienced and respected warrior. The colourful headdress in this project is decorated with brightly coloured paints, beads and feathers. When you wear it, you will feel like the chief of your tribe.

YOU WILL NEED

Large and small feathers
Coloured beads • String
Single corrugated cardboard
Paper pulp • Newspaper • Balloon
Small bowl • White emulsion paint
Coloured acrylic paint • Palette
Paintbrush • Sponge • Scissors
Pencil • Masking tape

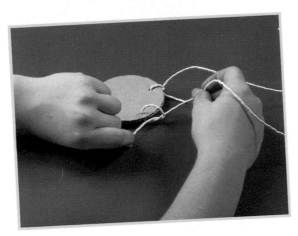

1 Use scissors to cut out the shape of the headdress shown on page 31 from single corrugated cardboard (see page 14, step 1 for instructions). Pierce two holes in each disc shape with the end of a paintbrush. Thread a length of string through each hole and tie to secure.

2 Cover one side of the cardboard with pulp. Leave the corrugations along the top of the cardboard shape uncovered as you will later stick feathers into these. Add a little more pulp over the circular disk shapes. Roll out a sausage of pulp and press this along the headdress to create a raised zig-zag decoration.

3 Blow up a balloon to approximately the same size as your head. Use masking tape to attach the balloon to a small bowl. Tie the headdress around the balloon and leave to dry for forty-eight hours.

4

Prime the headdress with white emulsion. When dry, decorate with zig-zags and dots of coloured acrylic paint.

FURTHER IDEAS
Paint the headband with earthy colours and use natural feathers for a different effect.

 5 Sponge the lengths of string with coloured paint. When dry, thread the strings at the bottom with coloured beads. Leave the strings at the side un-beaded, so you can tie the headdress around your head.

6 Push large coloured feathers into the holes along the top of the corrugated card, then tape two small feathers down each side.

Mexican Bowl

The inspiration for this bright little bowl comes from Mexico.
In fact, the art of pot-making originated from the Mexican area
as there was a lot of clay in the soil. Mexicans use bright colours
and geometric designs to decorate their craft work. In this
project, paper pulp is used to make a textured bowl. You can
use any bowl as a mould for this project (ceramic, plastic or glass)
and it does not matter what size it is. Remember that the finished papier
mâché bowl is intended to be decorative – you cannot eat out of it!

YOU WILL NEED
Selection of coloured beads
60cm (24in) of leather thong
Bowl • Clingfilm • Paper pulp
Newspaper • White emulsion paint
Coloured acrylic paint
Paintbrush • Palette
Cooling rack

1

Line the inside of a bowl with clingfilm.
Press paper pulp into the bowl with your
fingers. When it is about 1cm (½in) thick,
smooth the surface with your fingers.

2 Use the end of a paintbrush to
make holes around the bowl. Try
to make the spaces between the
holes roughly equal. Leave to dry
for three hours.

3 Carefully lift the pulp shell out of the bowl
using the clingfilm. Place on a cooling rack
then leave to dry for at least twenty-four hours.

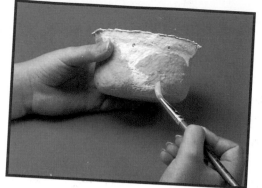

Prime the bowl with two coats of white emulsion paint. Leave to dry. Paint the outside of the bowl with coloured acrylic paint. Leave to dry.

5 Paint the inside of the bowl a different colour. Leave to dry.

6

Tie a knot in the length of thong and attach three beads. Thread it through one of the holes in the bowl. Tie a knot on the inside then cut off the end of the thong. Repeat around the bowl using the rest of the thong.

FURTHER IDEAS
Use a needle and cotton to thread dried melon or sunflower seeds on to your bowl.

Gothic Mirror

Gothic architecture sparked off the idea for this mirror. If you visit an old church and look at the pointed arches and carved stonework you will soon see the similarities. The mirror in this project is created using a mirror tile on a cardboard base. I have covered the cardboard with paper pulp to create a stone brickwork effect.

1 Cut out the frame shape shown on page 30 from double corrugated card (see page 14). Coat both sides with diluted PVA glue then allow to dry on a cooling rack.

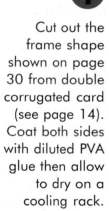

2 Apply two layers of pasted newspaper strips to the front and back of the frame. Leave to dry for four hours.

3 Apply PVA glue to the back of the mirror and then press it into place on the frame.

4 Press paper pulp on to the front and edges of the cardboard frame. Smooth the pulp with your fingers as you work.

5 While the pulp is still wet, use the long edge of a ruler to press horizontal lines into the pulp. Use the short edge of the ruler to create vertical lines. This will give the effect of stone brickwork. Leave to dry for forty-eight hours.

6 Paint the frame with natural-coloured paint then polish the mirror with a soft cloth.

Note If the frame starts to warp while the paper pulp is drying, place something heavy on the mirror tile – this will help flatten the frame.

FURTHER IDEAS
Make the mirror frame Norman rather than Gothic by cutting out a rounded arch.

Egyptian Cat

The Ancient Egyptians worshipped the cat goddess, Bastet, and made bronze cat figures dedicated to her. Bastet represented the power of the sun to ripen crops. This project uses a plastic bottle and a polystyrene ball as a base for re-creating Bastet. Pulp is used to model her features and, once painted, she is sponged with metallic paint to make her look like a real goddess.

1 Remove the bottle cap and place the polystyrene ball on top of the bottle. Tape the ball into place with long strips of masking tape. Press the tape flat on to the bottle to create a smooth finish.

2 Cover the polystyrene ball with a layer of paper pulp. Build up the nose then model two triangles of pulp to create the ears. Smooth the pulp with your fingers as you work.

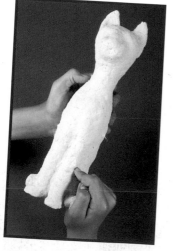

3 Work down the bottle, covering it with pulp. Build up the front legs and feet then the hind legs and feet using pulp. Neaten the base of the bottle then leave to dry for two days.

4 Paint the cat with coloured acrylic paint. Leave to dry. Paint in the eyes and nose in a darker colour.

6 Pour a little metallic paint on to a palette. Lightly sponge the cat all over.

5 Paint in the collar with coloured and metallic paint then leave to dry. Glue on a strip of ribbon around the top of the collar.

FURTHER IDEAS

Look for a picture of the Egyptian god, Anubis, who is represented as a jackal. Try creating a model of its head.

Aztec Necklace

Aztec craftsmen made beautiful jewellery. They considered jade to be their most precious stone, but they also used onyx, rock crystal and turquoise. The necklace in this project is made out of pulp which has been decorated with string, foil and metallic paint.

YOU WILL NEED
Foil • String
Paper pulp • Newspaper
Clingfilm • Cardboard
Coloured and metallic acrylic paint
White emulsion paint • Paintbrush
Sponge • PVA glue
Paste brush • Masking tape
Cooling rack

1 Tape a piece of clingfilm over a piece of card so that it is stretched tight.

2 Model a rectangle and a triangle of pulp then press each shape on to the clingfilm, flattening them with your fingers.

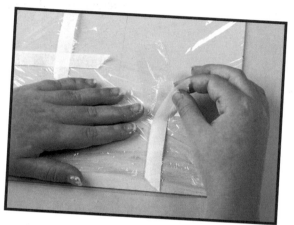

3 Press string into each pulp shape to create swirling patterns.

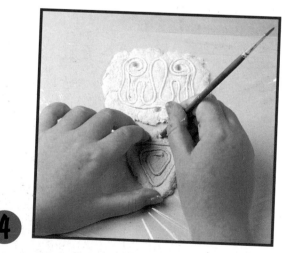

4 Use the end of a paintbrush to create two holes in the top corners and one in the bottom of the rectangular piece. Make one hole at the top of the triangle. Leave to dry for an hour. Carefully remove the shapes from the clingfilm then lay them on a cooling rack and leave to dry for a further twelve hours.

6

Sponge a length of string with metallic paint. Cut off a short piece and use this to link the rectangle and triangle together. Tie two longer pieces of string on to the rectangle so that you can do the necklace up.

5 Prime both pieces with white emulsion. Leave to dry then paint with acrylic paint in colours of your choice. Leave to dry, then lightly sponge with metallic paint. Roll two small balls of foil then glue one on to each piece.

FURTHER IDEAS

Model round pieces of pulp and attach earring clips to the back to make earrings. Thread round shapes with string to create a bracelet.

Roman Box

Roman city houses were often plain on the outside, but on the inside they were painted with scenes from mythology or the countryside. Romans covered their floors with mosaics (pictures and patterns made up from small pieces of stone). This project shows you how to make a simple mosaic box using cardboard, paint and a potato stamp. I have varnished the finished piece with diluted PVA glue to make it look shiny.

YOU WILL NEED
Potato
Single corrugated cardboard
Newspaper • Wallpaper paste
Vegetable knife • Chopping board
White emulsion paint
Coloured acrylic paint
Paintbrush • Palette • PVA glue
Paste brush • Masking tape
Scissors

 Cut out four 12cm (4¾in) and two 14cm (5½in) squares from single corrugated cardboard. Now cut out one 11cm (4¼in) and one 4cm (1½in) square. Tape the four 12cm (4¾in) squares together with masking tape to form the sides of the box. Tape one 14cm (5½in) square to one end to create a base.

2 To make a lid, glue the 11cm (4¼in) square to the centre of the remaining 14cm (5½in) square. Leave to dry. Turn over and pierce through the centre of the larger square with the end of a paintbrush. Apply a blob of glue to the hole then push a corner of the 4cm (1½in) square into the hole. Secure with small pieces of masking tape.

Coat the box and lid with diluted PVA glue. Leave to dry then apply two layers of pasted newspaper strips to the box. Leave to dry for four hours. Prime the box with two coats of white emulsion. Leave to dry.

4 Cut a 1cm (½in) wide chip shape from a potato. Dab it into acrylic paint then use it to stamp the sides of the box.

It is best to cut the potato on a chopping board. Get an adult to help you do this as vegetable knives are very sharp.

5 Stamp three rows of squares around the lid then paint the handle.

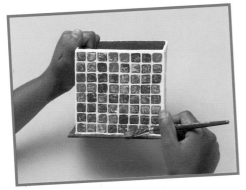

6 Paint the rim of the base and the inside of the box. Leave to dry then apply a coat of diluted PVA glue to varnish the outside of the box and the lid.

FURTHER IDEAS
Cut triangular and rectangular shaped potato shapes and use these to stamp a different design on to your box.

African Pencil Pot

The inspiration for this project comes from African drums. I have used cardboard tubing to recreate the cylindrical drum shapes and have decorated the pencil pot with colours typical of African art. It is best to use different sizes of cardboard tubing. You can make a simple pencil pot using just a few tubes, or you can use lots to create a more complicated one.

YOU WILL NEED
Cardboard tubing • Thin card
Newspaper • Wallpaper paste
PVA glue • Coloured acrylic paint
White emulsion paint • Sponge
Small paintbrush • Palette
Masking tape • Scissors
Pencil

1

Cut out five different lengths of cardboard tubing. Tape the tubes together, making sure that the bases are level. Place the tubes on a piece of thin card and draw around the bases. Cut around this shape then attach it to the bottom of the tubes using masking tape.

3

Prime the pencil pot with white emulsion paint then leave to dry. Apply a coat of coloured acrylic paint. When dry, paint coloured lines down each tube and a zig-zag border around the base. Leave to dry.

2 Apply two layers of newspaper strips over the pencil pot then allow to dry for four hours.

5 Paint a dark border around the base of the pencil pot, and add small triangles within the larger coloured ones.

6 Paint a dark band around the top of each tube then allow to dry. Finally, use the same colour to paint the inside of the tubes.

4 Dip a toothbrush into diluted acrylic paint, then hold it over the pencil pot and pull back the bristles with your finger. This will create a spattered paint effect. Wash your hands immediately afterwards.

FURTHER IDEAS
Create a completely different look by decorating with spots and stars instead of stripes and triangles.

Patterns

You can photocopy the patterns on these pages and then transfer the designs on to cardboard (see page 8). Use them the size that they appear here, or make them larger or smaller on a photocopier if you wish.

Get an adult to help you photocopy the patterns.

Pattern for the Gothic Mirror featured on pages 20–21.

*Pattern for the Indian Frame
featured on pages 14–15.*

*Pattern for the Native American
Headdress featured on pages 16–17.*

Index

Anubis 23

architecture 20

balloon 16

Bastet 22

beads 4, 7, 17, 19

bowl 18–19

box 26–27

bracelet 25

buttons 13

card 4, 6, 7, 8, 12, 14, 16, 20, 24, 26, 28, 30

cat 22–23

church 20

clingfilm 6, 9, 18, 24

colander 6, 10

cooling rack 6, 8, 18, 20, 24

craft knife 7, 8, 14

cutting 7, 8

drums 28

drying 6, 8, 10

earrings 25

feathers 4, 7, 17

foil 4, 7, 14, 25

frame 14–15

glass droplets 7, 13

goblet 12–13

headdress 16–17

layering 6, 9, 14, 20, 26, 28

leather thong 7, 19

masking tape 7, 12, 16, 22, 26, 28

mirror 20–21

mosaics 26

necklace 24–25

newspaper 4, 6, 8, 9, 10, 14, 20, 26, 28

paint 6

paintbrush 6, 16, 18, 24, 26

painting 11, 13, 17, 19, 21, 22, 23, 27, 28, 29

palette 6, 23

paste brush 6

pebbles 13

pencil 7

pencil pot 28–29

photocopying 30

plastic bottle 4, 12, 22

polystyrene ball 22

polythene 8

potato 6, 27

priming 6, 11, 19, 26, 28

pulp 6, 10, 12, 13, 16, 18, 20, 21, 22, 24

PVA glue 6, 8, 9, 10, 11, 13, 14, 20, 26, 27

recycling 4

ribbon 7, 23

ruler 7, 21

sari 14

scissors 7, 8

seeds 19

sieve 6, 10

spattering 29

sponge 6

sponging 14, 17, 23, 25

stamping 6, 27

string 4, 7, 15, 16, 17, 24, 25

Taj Mahal 14

tissue paper 15

toothbrush 6, 29

transferring a design 8

varnish 4, 6, 11

vegetable knife 7, 27

wallpaper paste 6, 9, 10

warping 8, 21

work surface 6, 8